Rad Sports

Rock Sport Climbing
Techniques and Tricks

Edward Willett

the rosen publishing group's
rosen
central

Published in 2003 by The Rosen Publishing Group, Inc.
29 East 21st Street, New York, NY 10010

First Edition

Library of Congress Cataloging-in-Publication Data

Willett, Edward, 1959–
Rock sport climbing: techniques and tricks / by Edward Willett.— 1st ed.
    p. cm. — (Rad sports)
Summary: Describes the basics, techniques, gear, safety aspects, and competitions of rock climbing.
Includes bibliographical references (p.   ) and index.
ISBN 0-8239-3847-6 (lib. bdg.)
1. Rock climbing—Juvenile literature. [1. Rock climbing.] I. Title. II. Series.
GV200.2 .W55 2003
796.9—dc21

2002007649

Manufactured in the United States of America

CONTENTS

Introduction

For most people, rocks are just rocks. Soaring granite cliffs are something to be photographed, then forgotten. Giant boulders fallen from a mountain top are nuisances you have to walk around when you're hiking. And mountains are something whose peaks you visit only if a ski lift or road can take you there.

Other people think the opposite. For them, every granite cliff is a challenge. They look at it and see every crack and bump. They try to figure out how they could get to the top using just their hands and feet. Giant boulders are things to climb over, not walk around. And mountain peaks are only worth visiting if they personally climb every foot of elevation to get there.

Those people are rock climbers, and there are hundreds of thousands of them all over the world. Climbing may be the hardest thing they've ever done. Their physical and mental abilities may be tested to their maximum limit. This is what they want. They have discovered that rock climbing is the most exciting and rewarding sport they have ever done.

Maybe you have what it takes to be a climber, too. Have you looked at cliffs, rocks, and mountains with an urge to climb them? Have you watched people scaling the climbing wall at your local gym? If so, then there is no reason for you not to get into this exciting sport. Like everything else worth doing, it takes training, practice, and dedication to do well—and do it safely! It's also a sport that's open to anyone, of any age.

This book will tell you about the different kinds of rock climbing, the equipment used in climbing, how you can get started climbing, and some basic climbing techniques. Once you've read it, you'll have a better idea if climbing is a sport for you—and you'll be all set to find a good instructor and start climbing for real.

All set? Then get roped up, and let's get started!

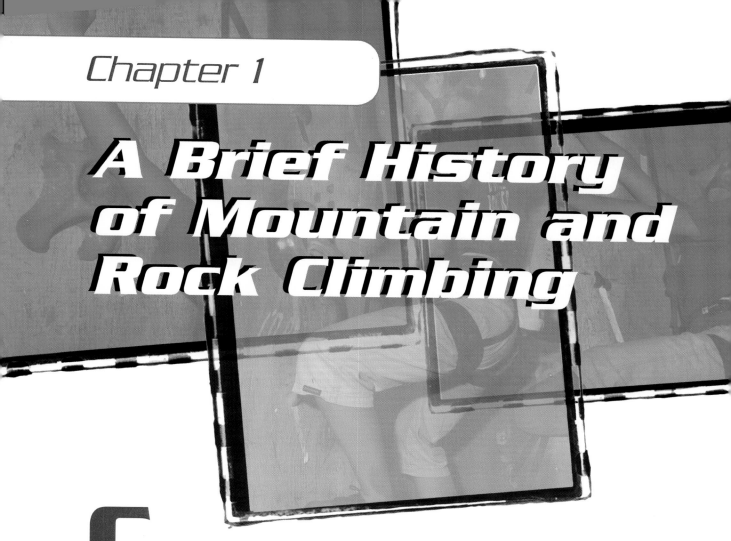

Chapter 1

A Brief History of Mountain and Rock Climbing

Climbing has been around in one form or another for as long as people have needed to travel. The ancient Greeks and Romans climbed mountains because they lay on important trade routes. Six hundred years ago, the Incas were climbing 20,000-foot mountains in the Andes to build religious altars and perform burials.

Climbing for Sport

The modern age of climbing began in 1786. That's when two Frenchmen, Michel-Gabriel Paccard and Jacques Balmat, made it to the top of Mont Blanc in France. At 15,771 feet (4,807 meters), Mont Blanc is the tallest mountain in the Alps. (Its name means "White Mountain," and it got that name because it is covered with ice year-round.) Paccard and Balmat's success launched what is often called the golden age of climbing. For about a hundred years afterward, many other climbers attempted to reach the top of other mountains in the Alps.

The first mountaineering club, called the Alpine Club, formed in 1857. By the middle of the 1860s, more than 200 of Europe's tallest mountains had been climbed. Most of the climbers were Britons using local guides.

The nineteenth century also showed the dangers of mountaineering. One of the peaks everyone wanted to be the first to climb was the 14,691-foot (4,478-meter) Matterhorn. This towering peak is located in the Alps on the border between Italy and Switzerland. In 1865, a party of Englishmen led by Edward Whymper successfully climbed it, beating a French team to the

Throughout the 1800s, local people and travelers hired guides to take them climbing in the mountains of Europe. These climbers often had only a single rope tied to them for safety.

summit. On the way down, however, two members of the party, Douglas Hadow and Lord Francis Douglas, as well as the party's guide, Michel Croz, fell to their deaths. The accident made headlines across Europe.

Early climbers climbed mountains wearing hobnailed boots (nails driven into the soles). They carried wooden staffs and used hemp rope for the toughest parts of a climb. Their success is all the more amazing when you consider hobnailed boots provide very little traction on rock. And hemp rope frays easily and snaps when a sudden strain is placed on it.

The World's Highest Peaks

In the twentieth century, climbers began to attempt the very highest mountains in the world. The Himalaya Mountains in Asia have the three highest peaks. In 1953, Edmund Hillary of New Zealand and Sherpa Tenzing Norgay of Nepal were the first people documented to climb the tallest mountain in the world: 29,028-foot (8,847-meter) Mount Everest. The following year 28,252-foot (8,611 m) K2, located in Pakistan in the Karakorum mountain range of the Himalayas, was summited by Achille Compagnoni and Lino Lacedelli of Italy. The third-highest mountain, 28,169-foot (8,585-meter) Kanchenjunga, was climbed the year after that by George Band and Joe Brown of England. (Actually, they stopped a few yards short of the summit out of respect for the local people, who consider the summit sacred.)

Rock Sport Climbing

Rock climbing started as a way of practicing the techniques needed to climb mountains. Rock climbers didn't try to reach mountaintops all the time. Those they did summit were only a few thousand feet high. Climbers practiced to build body strength and learn how to climb the bigger mountains.

Eventually rock climbing became its own sport. People found climbing cliff faces and small mountains more exciting and less dangerous than scaling full mountains. They could also be climbed in much less time. In addition to those reasons, rock climbers didn't have to travel halfway around the world to participate in the sport. They could find a small mountain or cliff face close to home.

Important Firsts in Climbing History

1786—First ascent of Mont Blanc (15,771 feet/4,807 meters) in France, the highest mountain in the Alps.

1811—First ascent of the "unclimbable" Jungfrau (13,642 feet/ 4,158 meters) in Switzerland.

1857—The first mountaineering club, the Alpine Club, is formed.

1865—First ascent of the Matterhorn (14,691 feet/4,478 meters) on the Swiss-Italian border.

1889—First ascent of Kilimanjaro (19,341 feet/5,895 meters) in Tanzania, the highest mountain in Africa.

1897—First ascent of Aconcagua (22,832 feet/6,959 meters) in Argentina, the highest mountain in South America.

1913—First ascent of Mount McKinley (20,322 feet/6,194 meters) in Alaska, the highest mountain in North America.

1925—First ascent of Mount Logan (19,850 feet/6,050 meters) in Yukon Territory, the highest mountain in Canada.

1953—First ascent of Mount Everest (29,028 feet/8,847 meters) in Nepal, the highest mountain in the world.

1954—First ascent of K2 (28,252 feet/8,611 meters) in Pakistan, the second-highest mountain in the world.

1958—First ascent of El Capitan in Yosemite National Park, the most famous rock face in the United States.

1978—Reinhold Messner becomes the first person to scale all fourteen of the world's peaks that are higher than 26,000 feet (7,924 meters).

Rock climbing really took off in the 1960s with the development of lightweight shoes, stronger ropes, and other devices to assist climbs. These advancements let climbers worry less about safety and more about style and technique. That, in turn, led to the surge in competitive rock climbing in the past fifteen years or so. An international World Cup circuit was formed in 1988.

Also in the 1980s, indoor climbing walls became popular. These are walls with handholds attached that allow climbers to practice their techniques indoors. Outdoor climbers use the indoor walls to stay in shape, but many people climb only on indoor walls for exercise and the thrill of the climb. Indoor or out, there's a style of climbing to suit anyone.

Other Styles of Climbing

Traditional. In traditional or "trad" climbing, you climb the rock using only your feet and hands. Removable safety devices are placed in the rock as you move higher. This is what most people think of as rock climbing.

Indoor climbing. Climbing indoors on a manufactured wall that has hand- and footholds bolted onto its face.

Bouldering. Climbing on large boulders and short walls. This climbing is usually done without a rope, since climbers are rarely more than ten feet (three meters) off the ground. Bouldering often involves very difficult moves and is both excellent practice and a sport in its own right.

Alpine climbing. Hiking combined with traditional rock or ice climbing.

Sport climbing. Climbing done on prebolted routes, usually over very difficult sections of rock.

Aid climbing. The kind of climbing necessary to scale many mountain peaks. Ropes and other aids are used not just for protection, but also to help climbers ascend.

Chapter 2

Equipment

Some rock-climbing styles require the use of equipment. You may not need to buy all your equipment when you begin taking lessons, because most trainers provide equipment. You will be climbing only with an instructor while taking lessons, and he or she will provide the ropes, harnesses, and other equipment you need.

If you continue to climb, you'll soon want to buy your own complete set of equipment. Be prepared to spend enough money to get top-quality stuff. Paying for the best is worth the money in terms of accident prevention.

Shoes

Modern climbing shoes are much more useful than the hobnail boots early mountaineers wore. Today's shoes have smooth soles made of stiff rubber. The rubber is tough enough to protect your foot from sharp rocks. It also supports your toes so they can hold your weight better. The smooth surface provides the maximum amount of friction between your feet and rocks. Since friction is what keeps the climber from sliding off the rocks, this is a very good thing. More than any other piece of equipment, modern climbing shoes have made accessible those stretches of rock people used to think couldn't be climbed.

Climbing shoes are lightweight and fit snugly. The rubber soles go over the toes and up the heel to provide the largest possible area for gripping rock.

When buying climbing shoes, make sure that they fit very snugly. You don't want your foot to slide around inside them. Climbing shoes are usually worn without socks and are usually a size or a size and a half smaller than your street shoes. This makes them uncomfortable to walk in, so if you have to hike a ways to reach the rocks you're going to climb, you'll want to wear a comfortable pair of hiking boots and carry your climbing shoes.

A pair of climbing shoes costs between $100 and $150. The best stores to buy them in are those that also have an indoor climbing wall. That way you can try out the shoes you are looking to buy. Take your time. The shoe should be tight (so it can stretch later without becoming loose) but not painful.

Helmets

The most important piece of safety equipment you'll wear is a helmet. Often when you're climbing, there will be other climbers above you. Those climbers may dislodge rocks or drop equipment. If either hits your head, you could be seriously injured or killed. There is also the danger of falling. While your rope and harness will catch you, you could swing into the cliff and hit your head. Again, this is bad news if you're not wearing a helmet.

Climbing helmets come in many different styles. You should always attach the chin strap for a snug fit before starting each climb.

Modern helmets are very lightweight. Your helmet should fit snugly and be comfortable. You should also be able to adjust it enough to fit a hat beneath it. That way, when you take your helmet off at the top of the climb, you'll have your hat to either keep you warm or protect you from the sun, depending on the weather. Bicycle helmets may look similar, but they don't offer the same protection. Make sure you get a proper climbing helmet.

Harnesses

Early mountaineers simply tied a rope around their waists and considered that protection enough. Early mountaineers died pretty often, too. Even if the rope held, a severe fall with the rope fastened that way could lead to a fractured spine or internal injuries.

A climbing harness helps prevent injury from slips or falls. The straps reach around each thigh and through the legs. These straps attach to the wide waist belt, which itself has metal loops used to attach to the climbing rope.

Climbers today wear harnesses. Harnesses are belts with loops for your legs. They're usually made out of wide nylon webbing, with lots of padding in the crotch. To "tie in" to a rope, you pass a loop of the rope through loops on the harness. A metal buckle fastens the harness around your waist. This part of the harness holds you when you fall. The belt has to be long enough to be doubled back through the buckle for a secure hold. Most harness buckles have a red stripe on them as a warning that you can see if you don't double back the belt. Climbers have a catchy phrase to remind them to double back the belt: "See red and you're dead."

The harness must fit snugly around your waist, just above your hipbones. The leg loops distribute your weight over your thighs and rear end. This makes being supported by the rope more comfortable. If you fall, it also protects you from injury. More expensive harnesses have more padding. Some also have adjustable leg loops. Harnesses cost between $30 and $80.

Climber's rope is made in two parts. The core (kern) is a single-piece nylon braid *(left)*. The outer sheath (mantle) is also a single-piece nylon braid, used to protect the core from fraying. Rope can be purchased in different lengths, but not usually longer than 165 feet (50 meters) so that it can be bundled easier for carrying.

Rope

The hemp rope that frayed or snapped easily in the early years of climbing has been replaced today with manufactured rope. Nylon rope is now the standard for all types of rock climbing. Climbing ropes are made using the "kernmantle" method. This consists of continuous braided nylon fibers, called the kern, surrounded by a continuous braided nylon outer sheath, called the mantle. Most of the rope's strength is in the kern. The mantle protects the kern from fraying and from the effects of weather.

Not only is modern climbing rope stronger than the old hemp rope, it's also a bit stretchy. This is important in the event of a fall. A sudden jerk exerts more force on a falling climber. This can injure the climber. The little bit of stretchiness in the nylon rope makes the stop more gentle.

Climbing ropes are usually about a quarter of an inch in diameter (much thinner than the old hemp ropes) and about 165 feet (50 meters) long. A climbing rope of that length costs between $100 and $200.

Carabiners

Carabiners (usually just called "biners" by climbers) are metal rings used for holding rope during a climb. Carabiners are either oval or D-shaped, with a spring-loaded gate that allows them to be opened. The spring normally holds the gate closed, but pressure on it opens it. This allows you to slip a rope inside the ring.

Carabiners are made of solid aluminum alloy. Most will hold about 2.2 tons (1,995 kilograms) without breaking. Carabiners come in both locking and non-locking varieties. Locking carabiners have a sheath that covers the gate. The sheath may screw into place or have a spring to hold it in place. This makes it less likely that the gate will open unexpectedly. However, locking biners can't easily be used one-handed. They also take longer to use. This makes them most useful for situations where you have both hands available and aren't in a hurry. Carabiners are the most inexpensive piece of climbing equipment. A basic carabiner costs only $5 or $6. Some fancier models cost a few dollars more.

Carabiners are a climber's basic lifeline between the rock wall and the rope. The spring-loaded gate opens *(left)* for easy attachment. The gate locks easily into place *(right)* for safety.

Belay Devices

A belay device uses friction to stop a rope from slipping. Climbers use belay devices to prevent themselves from falling long distances.

Belay devices help one climber stop (belay) the fall of a fellow climber by applying friction against the rope to which the falling climber is attached. Belay devices don't clamp onto the rope automatically to stop a falling climber. Instead, they assist the climber "on belay" (the one responsible for stopping falls). He or she stops the fall by pulling back on the rope to create a ninety-degree bend against a post in the device. Belay devices make it possible to stop falls using far less strength than was once required.

How Safe Is That Rope?

Ropes are tested by the International Mountaineering and Climbing Federation, or Union Internationale des Associations d' Alpinisme (UIAA). To test ropes, the UIAA attaches a 176-pound (80-kilogram) block to the end of a nine-foot piece of the rope. The rope is fed through a carabiner, then attached to an anchor. The weight is raised as high as it can go and dropped at least five times. This is a far harder fall than any rope would have to withstand in climbing. One climber compared it to attaching a cow to a rope and marching it off of a 300-foot (91-meter) cliff.

Protection

"Protection" (often shortened to "pro"), in climbing lingo, refers to objects that can be placed firmly into a rock and used for anchoring a rope. As a beginning climber, you won't be responsible for placing protection into rocks. However, unless you limit your climbing to an indoor wall, you will use protection as you climb.

There are two basic types of protection. Monolithic protection has no moving parts. Spring-loaded camming devices (SLCDs) have many moving parts. "Nuts," or "chocks," are one form of monolithic protection. They're tapered metal wedges that are inserted into a crack in a rock. A loop of steel cable attached to them provides an anchor for a climber. Placed properly, they're extremely strong.

Another type is the "hex," a hexagonal tube of aluminum that's about as wide as it is long, anywhere from less than half an inch (1.3 centimeters) to just over two inches (five centimeters) A strong piece of cord, tied into a loop, runs through two pairs of little holes on opposite sides of the hex.

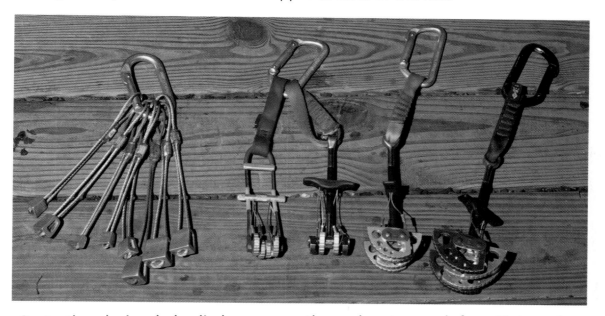

Protection devices help climbers secure themselves to a rock face. Nuts and chocks *(left)* have no moving parts. Climbers secure the metal wedges into cracks and secure carabiners in the looped cable. Spring-loaded camming devices *(center and right)* have moving parts to secure themselves in larger cracks or holes.

SLCDs consist of a stem with an axle at one end that holds four spiral-shaped spring-loaded cams (wheels able to expand or retract). With the cams retracted, the climber inserts the SLCD into a rock. Then he or she releases the cams, allowing them to spring back. When the SLCD is pulled downward by a fall, the spiral-shaped cams rotate and widen, forcing themselves harder against the rock.

SLCDs are easier to use than monolithic protection and can be used in a wider variety of cracks. However, monolithic protection is much cheaper—typically under $10 per piece, compared to $50 to $100 for an SLCD.

Climbers use chalk to keep their hands dry for a better grip.

Chalk

After all this high-tech talk about SLCDs and kernmantling, you might be surprised to learn that one of the most basic of all climbing supplies is plain old chalk. Chalk, or magnesium carbonate, helps keep your hands dry. This improves your grip on the rock. A block of chalk costs only a dollar or so. A bag to put it in that hangs from your belt might cost $15.

Do I Really Need All This?

Technically, you don't need all of this stuff to climb. What you need the equipment for is to protect yourself in the event of a fall. If you take up climbing, you will eventually fall. If you keep climbing, you'll fall many times. But it is possible to minimize the risk of a fall. It's also possible to fall without hurting yourself. Good climbers are safety-conscious at all times. Chapter 4 takes a closer look at climbing safety.

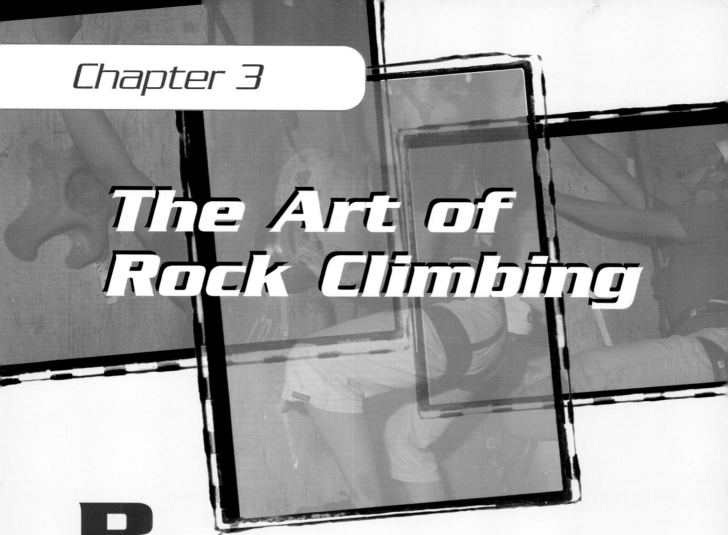

Chapter 3

The Art of Rock Climbing

By now you've probably figured out that rock climbing isn't something you just decide to do one day for fun. It's a sport that takes hours and hours of instruction and sometimes years of practice to become qualified for more technical climbs.

So how do you get started? Look in the yellow pages for a climbing gym. Call them up or pay them a visit and sign up for a beginner's course. They'll teach you the fundamentals of climbing, good climbing techniques, and proper safety procedures. Once you're a part of the local climbing scene, even as a beginner at the gym, you'll soon find out where you can turn for more advanced climbing instruction. You may decide to stick to the indoor climbing wall, or you may want to move outdoors. Either way, your beginning-level instructor can tell you where you can sign up for the next level of instruction you need.

Belaying 101

The basic element of safety for climbers is the belay. As a beginning climber, you won't be asked to belay others. You should know how it works, however, and always keep your eyes and ears open to learn from teachers and more experienced climbers.

Anywhere along the climb, it's the belayer's responsibility to halt the fall of his or her fellow climber if something goes wrong.

1. In a typical climb by two experienced climbers, the belayer first anchors herself to the ground with a good, two-footed balance.

2. The climber starts up the rock wall, using hand- and footholds as her path up the wall.

Climbing Techniques and Tips

Climbing on a wall is done with "top-roping." The first few times you climb outside you'll probably also be top-roped. In top-roping, the rope runs from the climber (you) through a secure anchor at the top of the climb, then back down to the ground where the belayer stands by to stop any fall. This is the safest possible way to climb, and allows you to learn how to move up the rock and use and trust the gear involved in climbing with a minimum amount of risk.

Don't use your arms to pull yourself up

Rock climbing shouldn't be that much different from climbing a ladder. Many beginners find that they fail in their climb because their arms give out. However, if you're climbing properly, most of the work of moving your body upward against the force of gravity should be done by your legs.

Keep your arms relatively straight *(left)*; this will stop you from using them to pull yourself up *(right)*. Some climbing gyms teach this by putting tubes on your elbows that force you to keep your arms straight while you climb.

Rest every few moves

Once your muscles wear out, you're stuck; you can't go any higher. Conserve your energy and give your muscles time to rebound. Hang from a straight arm while shaking out the other.

Don't over-grip with your hands

It's natural to grip every handhold as tight as you can when you're afraid of falling, but this will quickly exhaust the strength in your fingers. Just hold on as hard as you have to so that you do not slip.

Look down as you climb

You want to go up, not down, so why look down? For one thing, looking down as you climb *(left)* forces you to move away from the rock, which lets you use different muscles while resting others. Looking up *(right)* doesn't let you look for footholds. Your next foothold, after all, is probably going to be somewhere below your waist, not over your head!

Keep your hips over your feet

This adjusts your center of gravity and helps you keep your balance *(left)*. Push your hips away from the rock when it slopes forward. Pull your hips closer to the rock when it becomes more vertical.

Decide how you're going to grip the rock before you do so. Do the same with your feet. Don't move a foot until you know exactly where the next hold for it is. Then, watch your foot as you move it until it is on that hold. When your feet and hands are out of position *(right)*, you are unbalanced and using too much energy.

Basic Hand- and Footholds

There's more than one way to hang onto a rock with your hand. You also have more than one way to move up it with your feet. Following are some basic handholds.

The Wrap

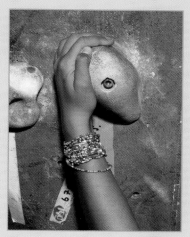

Use the wrap on knob-like projections. Wrap your hand around it like you would to grip a baseball.

The Crimp

Only your fingertips are in contact with the rock using the crimp hold. You use it on holds that are flat-topped and have small, sharp edges. It works, but it's painful. You can tell you're using a crimp grip if your knuckles are sharply lifted, forcing the fingers down.

The Open

Your fingers are loosely holding the rock in the open grip. Your grip is open if the knuckles are low and under the hold.

The Thumb Stack

The thumb stack is a crimp grip, with your thumb wrapped over the top two knuckles of your index and middle fingers for extra support.

The Pocket

The pocket can only hold a few fingers inside its hole. You'll run into these kinds of holds more often on indoor climbing walls, but you should also be prepared to run into them outdoors.

The Pinch

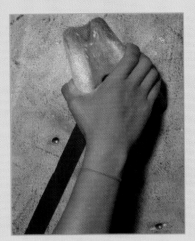

The pinch is done by squeezing a rock between your fingers and thumb. It's usually used on large holds, and requires a lot of hand and finger strength.

Footholds

Footholds aren't as varied as handholds. These three footholds work the best:

Inside Edge

Use the inside of your foot, at the base of the big toe. This is the strongest part of your foot and climbing shoe.

Outside Edge

Use the outside of your foot, at the base of the little toe. This part of your foot is weaker, but sometimes you have to use it, especially when moving side-ways across the rock (called "traversing").

Front Pointing

With the front of your shoe pointing against the wall, you stick your big toe into a hold. This foothold is tough on your toes.

Putting It Together: How To Scale a Wall

Most indoor climbing gyms can provide or rent equipment to you for a climbing session. Make sure you wear properly fitting climbing shoes and loose-fitting clothing before each climb. Likewise, belt yourself into your harness and follow your instructor or belayer's instructions.

Indoor climbing is top-roped. That means the rope goes from the ground up to the top of the wall, through an anchor, and back down the wall to you. You (or your instructor, the first few times) tie it onto your harness.

Your instructor or other partner will then belay you from the floor. The belayer pulls in the slack rope as you climb and stands ready to catch you so that, if you fall, you won't fall far.

Plan your route. Indoor walls, unlike outdoor walls, usually have handholds of different colors indicating the various routes to the top. The colors also indicate the difficulty of the route.

1. Once you know which handholds you'll use, begin to climb. Put one foot onto the lowermost hold and grip two higher holds with your hands.

2. Step up onto the lowermost hold. Remember to climb primarily with your legs, not your arms. Your legs are much stronger. Use your arms mainly to steady yourself, not to pull yourself up.

3

3. Use one hand, for example, to execute an open grip. Your other hand might be near enough to a pocket projection.

4

4. Pick your line as you move up the wall. Try a crimp or an open grip. You're really only holding on with your fingertips, but your hand is fairly flat against the bump and your knuckles are low.

5

5. Move your foot to the next hold. This is a pocket that is big enough for you to put your big toe into. This is called "front pointing" or "toeing in."

How to Scale a Wall
(continued)

6. If you get tired, use a resting technique. Hold on with one hand, lean back, and shake the free arm.

7. Sometimes you may want to use a double grip. This photo shows a double open grip. Pull yourself up to the next foothold now.

8. If you have to change your line up the wall, you'll want to move sideways, or traverse the wall. To move to your right, set the outside of your left foot and the inside of your right foot against the wall. Use your hands for a single or double grip and move over.

9. The higher you climb, the more nervous you might get. Don't be. Your body is secure. Keep climbing on the line you've chosen. Rest when necessary. Maintain your center of gravity with your body over your legs.

10. Concentrate on footholds as well as handholds and remember to climb with your legs, not your arms. Once you reach the top, you can either climb down or simply step off the wall and be lowered by your belayer.

Practice, Practice, Practice

In case you haven't figured it out yet, the key to learning to climb (or do anything else) is practice, practice, practice. Once you've learned the proper climbing technique from your instructor, you can continue to practice on the indoor climbing wall. Just like with the great outdoors, indoor climbs come in various levels of difficulty, so as your skills improve, there's always another challenge waiting for you. If you'd like to practice your skills outdoors, a good place to begin is with bouldering. Working on rocks just a few feet off the ground allows you to improve your climbing technique without as much worry about safety.

Chapter 4

Safety

Unless you stick to bouldering, rock climbing is eventually going to find you far enough above the ground that you could be seriously hurt or even killed if you fell. That's where much of the thrill of rock climbing comes from. And falling isn't the only risk rock climbers face. Climbing often takes place in mountainous wilderness areas. These areas pose their own dangers, from dangerous wildlife (bears, cougars, snakes) to unpredictable weather.

Safety, therefore, begins with having safe equipment. Climbers should be wary of using second-hand rope, harnesses, or other equipment. If you're going to entrust your life to your equipment, it's worthwhile to make sure you have the best you can buy.

The best equipment in the world won't help you if you misuse it, however. An expensive SLCD that's improperly inserted into a rock will pop out if you fall, no matter how much you paid for it. If you don't double back the belt through the buckle of your harness, your harness may come off in a fall. And even that thoroughly tested, high-tech climbing rope will fail if you let it rub long enough against the sharp edge of a rock.

If a baseball player's bat breaks, no big deal. If a climber's rope breaks, it could be deadly—and maybe threaten others depending on the same rope. So it's important to learn to climb from top-notch instructors. They know how to use the equipment safely, and they can teach students willing to learn.

Talking the Talk

There's usually not a lot of chattering during a climb. Everyone is working too hard to talk. There are a few phrases you'll hear and should learn.

Belay on! The belayer calls this out when everything is ready. The belayer now has the responsibility to catch the leader in case of a fall.

Climbing! An acknowledgment that the belay is in place and the leader is beginning to climb.

Slack! The leader wants more rope paid out.

Rope! The leader wants more rope taken up.

Off belay! The leader has reached the end of the climb, is in a safe spot, and will soon be belaying the original belayer up the climb. The belayer is now free to stop belaying and remove the rope from the belaying device.

Belay off! What the belayer yells when the rope has been removed from the belaying device.

Watch me! A signal that the leader is about to attempt something that carries a real risk of falling.

Falling! The leader has come off the rock.

Rock! Something—a rock or a piece of equipment—is heading down. Watch out!

Fitness for Climbers

If something does go wrong on a climb, it's going to take strength and stamina to deal with it. You're also more likely to make sound decisions as you climb if you're not so too tired and in pain that all you can think about is your discomfort. That makes getting in shape something you can do to make your climbing safer. It will also make it easier and more enjoyable!

You should establish a good basic fitness routine that builds cardiovascular and muscular endurance. Running and cycling are good choices. Stretching exercises that enhance flexibility are a must, too. Strength training can also help. Climbing uses every muscle in your body, so a good overall weight program will help. Eventually, though, you'll want to work on the muscles that are used the most in climbing: those in the arms, hands, shoulders and elbows. Pull-ups are one good exercise to work into your routine.

Indoor Walls as Fitness Tools

The best way to build the muscles needed for climbing is by climbing. This is where the indoor climbing wall is useful even for outdoor climbers. It's the best place to build the muscles you need to safely meet the challenges of outdoor rock faces.

The attached hand- and footholds on indoor walls save climbers time. Climbers can focus on practicing different handholds (see chapter 3) or arm/leg climbing techniques. Indoor walls also let climbers practice more technical climbs. For instance, vertical climbs and overhangs require special techniques and a lot of strength and stamina. Practicing these on an indoor wall lets climbers make mistakes without suffering dangerous consequences.

Muscles and Climbing

All this talk about fitness and muscles brings up some questions. Must a person be a musclebound monster to climb? Or, at the other extreme, should he or she have the skinny, wiry build of a jockey?

You're Never Too Young

Youth is no barrier to being one of the world's top climbers. Katie Brown of Paris, Kentucky, started climbing when she was twelve. When she was fourteen (and weighed all of eighty-five pounds) she won the Junior National Championship and the Youth World Championship in sport climbing. The following year she won the ESPN X Games Sport Climbing Women's Difficulty competition. She's won many more competitions since.

Chris Sharma of Santa Cruz, California, also started climbing at age twelve. When he was fourteen he won the Bouldering Nationals in Phoenix. The next year he made his first 5.14c-rated climb—at the time, the toughest class of climb in the American rating system. If you have the skill and the will, you can be a top climber at any age.

The answer to both questions is no. Climbing is a sport that is open to everyone. You don't have to be a natural athlete, young, or in perfect physical condition. Many people don't start climbing until they are in their forties or even older. People with disabilities can climb; El Capitan has been climbed by a blind climber, and many people without legs are excellent climbers.

The goal of climbing is to do the best you can with what you have to work with. You may never be able to tackle certain rock faces. Nevertheless, the challenge you'll find on the rocks you can climb will be just as exhilarating to you as the challenges the best rock climbers in the world find on the world's hardest climbs.

Chapter 5

Competitive Climbing

Climbing has been called a sport throughout this book. For some people, though, a sport isn't a sport unless it involves competition. Where's the competition in rock climbing? Many climbers point out that the rock itself is the competition. You are competing against the rock and against yourself. You're competing against your own fatigue, your own fear, your own pain.

There is a form of climbing where you compete against other climbers, however. It's called competition climbing. Men and women compete in three categories: difficulty, speed, and bouldering. Bouldering is all about style. Speed is just what it implies: Whoever completes the climb fastest wins. Difficulty, however, is the most prestigious class. Time doesn't matter.

The winner is whichever climber gets to the highest hold on the route. Competition climbing usually takes place on prebolted routes.

Competition Climbing Federations

In the 1980s, climbing federations began to organize competitions with established rules and regulations. The first fully sanctioned competition took place at Lake Garda, Italy, in 1985, on a route set up on a steep rock face below an ancient citadel.

Climber Katie Brown negotiates an overhanging section during the Women's Climbing Difficulty competition at the 1997 X Games in San Diego, California.

Today, competition climbing has moved indoors. All official international competitions take place on premade walls. At first glance, the walls look impossible to climb. They often feature overhanging sections 15 or 20 feet (4.5 or 6 meters) away from the vertical wall. But the world's top climbers find ways to climb them.

The excitement of competitive climbing has been highlighted by its appearance as part of ESPN's X Games. If this style of climbing appeals to you, check with your local climbing gym. It probably holds its own local competitions. Once you think you're ready, enter one. Even if you decide afterward that competition climbing isn't what you want to concentrate on, the training and discipline it calls for will make you a better all-around climber.

And ultimately, that's what rock climbing is about. It's about doing the best you can do. It's about learning to trust your body and use your mind. It's about meeting a challenge head-on and pushing yourself to your limits. For dedicated climbers, rock climbing is more than just a sport; it's a way of life.

Glossary

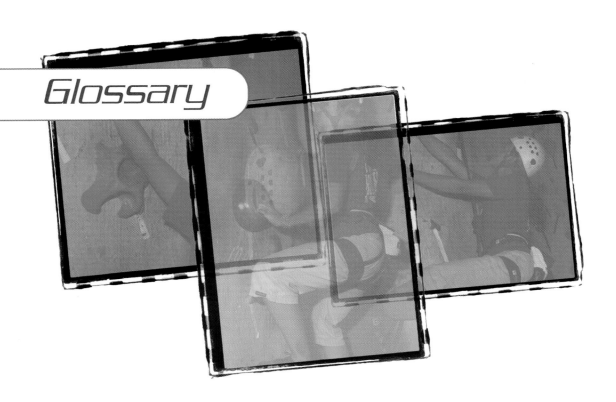

aid climbing Climbing in which fixed or placed protection supports the climber's weight and helps him or her climb.

anchor The point where rope is fixed to a rock. Anchors can be natural (trees, a spike of rock) or artificial (a bolt in the rock).

belay A safety technique in which a stationary climber stands ready to break the fall of an ascending partner.

belay device A metal device through which a climbing rope is threaded that helps a belayer apply friction to the rope in the event of a fall.

belayer The person who is ready to brake the rope should a climber fall.

biner Short for carabiner.

bolts Stout metal pins drilled into a rock to hold rope and provide permanent protection for climbers.

bouldering Climbing short, difficult routes on low-lying rocks without protective gear.

40

cam A mechanical spring-loaded device that can be inserted into cracks in the rock and to which a rope can be fixed.

carabiner Aluminum or steel oval or D-shaped devices with a spring-loaded gate through which a climbing rope can be threaded.

chalk Powdered magnesium carbonate. Climbers use it to dry sweaty hands.

crack A split or space in a rock that can be used as a foothold or handhold or a place to insert protection.

crimping Grasping a small hold with fingers tightly together and bent at the first knuckle.

free climbing Climbing without using artificial aids. (Ropes and anchoring devices are used for safety, but don't bear the weight of the climber during the climb or help with his or her upward progress.)

gumby A novice climber.

harness A device worn by climbers that allows them to attach themselves to a rope. Made of nylon webbing, it also distributes the force of a fall over more of the climber's body, lessening the risk of injury.

leading Climbing first, with no safety top-rope, placing protection as you go. This is the most dangerous form of climbing and requires skill and a trustworthy belayer down below.

locking carabiner A carabiner, the gate of which can be locked tight for increased security.

pro An abbreviation for protection.

protection Bolts or other gear placed into a rock that prevent a climber from falling too far.

route A path up a rock face or climbing wall.

sport climbing The climbing of routes that have pre-fixed protection, usually bolts.

spotter A bouldering partner who stands ready to help the climber control his or her landing in the event of a fall.

top-roping Climbing with the rope above you. You can be belayed either from the top or from the bottom of the climb.

traditional climbing Climbing in which climbers place their own protection, and in which the route taken is improvised during the ascent.

For More Information

The American Alpine Club

710 Tenth Street, Suite 100
Golden, CO 80401
(303) 384-0110
Web site: http://www.americanalpineclub.org

American Sport Climbers Federation

125 West 96th Street, Suite 1D
New York, NY 10025
(888) ASCF-ROX (272-3769)

Climbing Magazine

0326 Highway 133, Suite 190
Carbondale, CO 81623
(800) 493-4569
Web site: http://www.climbing.com

In Canada

Alpine Club of Canada

Indian Flats Road
P.O. Box 8040
Canmore, AB T1W 2T8
(403) 678-3200
Web site: http://www.alpineclubofcanada.ca

Association of Canadian Mountain Guides

Box 8341
Canmore, AB T1W 2V1
(403) 678-2885
Web site: http://www.acmg.ca

Web Sites

Due to the changing nature of Internet links, the Rosen Publishing Group, Inc., has developed an online list of Web sites related to the subject of this book. This site is updated regularly. Please use this link to access the list:

http://www.rosenlinks.com/rs/rsct/

For Further Reading

Brimmer, Larry Dane. *Rock Climbing*. Danbury, CT: Franklin Watts, 1997.

Champion, Neil. *Rock Climbing*. Crystal Lake, IL: Heineman Library, 1999.

Jeffries, David. *Rock Climbing and Mountaineering*. Austin, TX: Raintree Steck-Vaughn Publishers, 2002.

Long, Bob. *How to Rock Climb,* Third Edition. Evergreen, CO: Chockstone Press, 2000.

Nichols, John. *Sport Climbing*. Austin, TX: Raintree Steck-Vaughn Publishers, 2002.

Voeller, Edward A. *Sport Climbing*. Mankato, MN: Capstone Press, 2001.

Bibliography

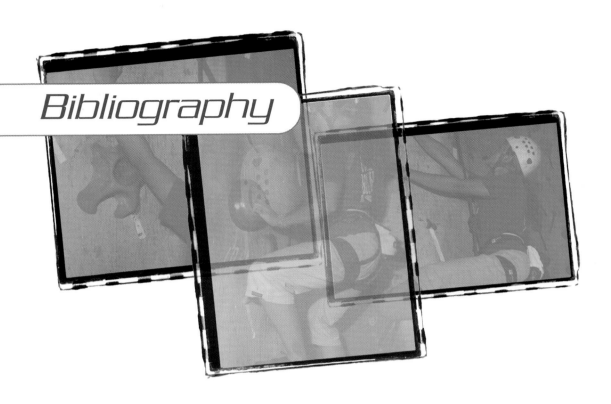

"Adventure Sports Online: Climbing." Retrieved May 5, 2002 (http://www.adventuresports.com/index/climbdir.htm).

CLIMB. Retrieved May 5, 2002 (http://climb.altabase.com).

Copp, Jonathan. "Rock Climbing 101." Great Outdoors Resource Page (GORP). Retrieved May 5, 2002 (http://www.gorp.com/gorp/activity/climb/skills/cli_101.htm).

Edwards, Stephen. "Rock Climbing Equipment and Techniques." Retrieved May 6, 2002 (http://www.alumni.caltech.edu/~sedwards/climbing/).

Jackenthal, Stefani, and Joe Glickman. *The Complete Idiot's Guide to Rock Climbing*. Indianapolis: Alpha Books, 2000.

Peakware World Mountain Encyclopedia. Retrieved May 6, 2002 (http://www.peakware.com/).

Trebisky, Tom. "Tom's Rock Climbing Info." Retrieved May 6, 2002 (http://kofa.as.arizona.edu/climbing/).

Index

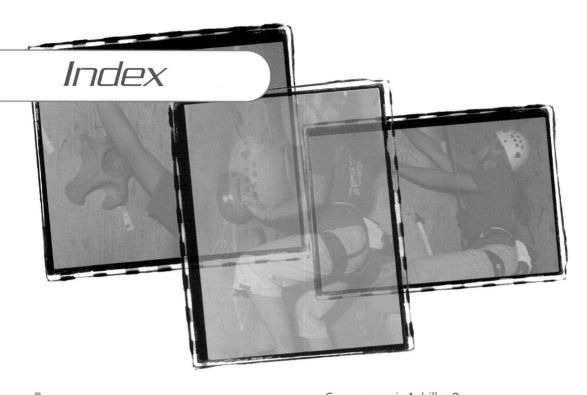

About the Author

Edward Willett is the author of more than twenty books, including young adult science fiction and fantasy novels, computer books, and nonfiction children's books on topics ranging from Ebola to careers in outer space. He also writes a weekly science column for newspapers and radio, hosts a TV show about computers, and is a professional actor and singer.

Ed lives in Regina, Saskatchewan, Canada, with his wife, Margaret Anne, and daughter, Alice. You can visit Ed online at www.edwardwillett.com.

Acknowledgments

Special thanks to Philadelphia Rock Gym, Oaks, PA.

Credits

Cover © Don Mason/Corbis; pp. 4–5 © Gavriel Jecan/Corbis; p. 8 © Hulton/Archive/Getty Images; pp. 13–20, 22–33 © Maura B. McConnell; p. 39 © AP/Wide World Photos.

Editor

Mark Beyer

Design and Layout

Les Kanturek